Why Are They Like That?
Blacks

*Questions you've dared to ask, answered
by real people, celebrities and experts*

A book series based on the award-winning
sharing project that's captured worldwide
attention helping people in their personal,
social and business relationships

Phillip J. Milano

For Robin, Jacob, Lucas and Ben

Publisher:
Y Forum
yforum@yforum.com

ISBN: 978-1-07-908856-4

Cover and interior layout by Sandy Weber,
Key 3 Creative, Jacksonville, Florida
Cover photo credit: Rawpixel. Stock photo for illustrative purposes only; any person depicted is a posed model.

Content based in part on the popular Y? sharing project and Dare to Ask column

Find out more about the author, upcoming books and speeches at www.phillipmilano.com, facebook.com/PhillipJMilano or @PhillipMilano.

Books In This Series

Why Are They Like That? Blacks

Why Are They Like That? Whites

Why Are They Like That? Hispanics

Why Are They Like That? Asians

Why Are They Like That? Gay Men

Why Are They Like That? Lesbians

Why Are They Like That? Women

Why Are They Like That? Men

Why Are They Like That? Rich and Poor

Why Are They Like That? Religious (or not)

Why Are They Like That? Disabled People

Why Are They Like That? Young and Old

Praise for the Y? sharing project and the book "I Can't Believe You Asked That!" (Perigee)

"Milano is quietly revolutionizing cross-cultural communication..."
- Pulitzer Prize-winning columnist Leonard Pitts

"If you've ever hesitated to ask a question because you think it might be considered insensitive or impolitic, now is your chance ... Nothing is considered out of bounds..."
- CNN Headline News

"(It) tells more about who we are and how we feel about each other than you're likely to learn from a dozen sociology texts…"
- Washington Post News Service

"Mr. Milano has dared to open the field of debate to the maximum…"
- Le Monde, Paris

"(A) remarkable contribution to cross-cultural understanding…"
- The (London) Guardian

"A truly rare achievement ... has the potential to have a profound impact on the way we all see and understand each other..."
- Playboy magazine

"It's an incredible book. It diffuses everything ... Nothing is off limits, and the questions have that childlike honesty to them..."
- Dee Snider, Twisted Sister; host, "Dee Snider Radio"

"A take-no-prisoners attitude prevails between the volume's covers . . . This book is hard to put down..."
- Midwest Book Review

"A+ (highest rating) ... Everything you wanted to know but were afraid to ask gets tackled here ..."
- Entertainment Weekly

CONTENTS

Introduction

Why Are They Like That? is a series of books based on an award-winning worldwide sharing project in which real people, experts and celebrities talk about things that make us different from each other. Silly things. Sad things. Funny things. Profound things.

Read with an open mind and we believe that by the time you're finished you'll have a much better understanding of how to make more and real friends, money and love. It's that simple.

Why? Because this isn't about trying to get ahead with diversity training. We are well beyond that. According to the Census Bureau, by 2050 the United States will have no racial or ethnic minority.

No, this is about moving past talking about how to understand each other to talking to each other. Right now.

That's why there's no agenda to these books other than getting the conversation going. We can discuss studies and methods for elevating social consciousness all we want, but there is no substitute for real dialogue.

That's where Why Are They Like That? stands apart from other books on the topic. You will see how people talk about their real differences of race, religion, sex, disability and more.

The success of the approach is proven: It's based on the ground-breaking Y? website project, blog and column that have attracted millions of visitors and worldwide media attention.

Our hope is that by reading, you will become more comfortable asking and answering the questions yourself, expecting the unexpected in return and helping change the ground rules for how we learn from and about each other. To that end, we wrap up each book in the series with our O.U.T.L.O.U.D. Method for Dialogue, with tips to help you get your own conversations started. Ultimately, that is what this effort is all about.

After all, if you want to make more friends, money and love, you better know the people you're talking to, selling to or opening to. Knowledge isn't just power. It's all power.

Enjoy.

Phillip J. Milano
Founder, Y?

Who's that wearing slippers in public, you say?

They asked:

Why do I constantly see black people shopping in stores with their slippers on?

— Julie, 27, Akron, Ohio

You said:

And why do whites go into public with no shoes on?

— Jimia, Grand Blanc, Mich.

I've seen white college kids wander around in PJs on campus, but it seems like the majority of people who shop in slippers are black.

— Mary C., white female, Toronto

I work in a grocery store and see white people do this all the time.

— Grant, Sierra Vista, Ariz.

I am white and have been known to wear not only slippers but my jammies to the grocery store. It's not just a "black thing."

— Maureen, Pittsburgh

We found:

Our stakeouts of Whole Foods, camping supply stores, slow-food farm tours and non-dance hall reggae concerts turned up no swarms of whites donning slippers. Likewise, high-def satellite images of un-whole grocers, indoor event suppliers, faster-food locales and a few Tyler Perry movies did not find them overrun with blacks in casual morning footsies.

Yet the blacks-wearing-slippers stereotype persists. Even former President Barack Obama took a media hit for urging a black audience to "take off your bedroom slippers, put on your marching shoes."

Who ... huh? We decided to ask the experts.

"I've never seen blacks wearing slippers," offered Norine Dresser, a folklorist who's white and wrote the "Multicultural Manners" column for the Los Angeles Times for years. "My only guess would be that if this occurs, it might have to do with the high percentage of diabetes in the African-American community, which can cause foot problems."

Also, people overall just seem to be more "relaxed" nowadays, she said.

"I once did a book that had a cultural reference to Madonna going out in a bustier and my editor objected, saying that was just a fad. Well, guess what? People are wearing all sorts of undergarments out now."

Meanwhile, KnightKrawler, a spoken-word artist and cultural commentator, said that in "certain neighborhoods," he does see slippers worn more often by his fellow blacks.

"They might think, 'Well, I'm just going to put them on for a quick run out of the house', but they end up going and getting the paper, then a haircut ... all of a sudden they end up in Target."

He even sees them worn by the retail cashiers he supervises, sending them home after they tell him they "forgot, or just want to be comfy."

Does it mean they're less refined than whites? Not when white people are sticking their bare feet out their car windows all the time.

"It's beyond age or race, it's just preferences for comfort. I wouldn't go out with slippers, but it's not a societal breakdown. It's people having an 'I don't give a damn' moment."

Her little boy is a little misguided (and afraid) of black people

They asked:

I've always taught my 4-year-old son that people are people, regardless of skin color. His father isn't the most tolerant person, but he's never taught my son anything to the contrary. So it surprised me in the supermarket when my son pointed at a black man and told me to not go near because "they are the enemy." What should I do?

— *Amanda, 21, white, Louisville, Ky.*

You said:

By keeping him under your wing and teaching him proper ethics and morals, he will be OK. Praise and love him and be there for him. The same ethics and morals that got you where you are should be the same for him.

— *Bruce, 49, white, Newark, N.J.*

Ask him who told him that, because someone did. Let's hope it's not his father, since then you'll have a difficult time limiting his exposure to such poison.

— *CWayne, Parsippany, N.J.*

Someone is teaching him these things. A 4-year-old doesn't spontaneously decide blacks are the "enemy" on his own. If it's not [the parents], look at relatives, and/or neighbors and neighbors' kids. Oh, and making a huge deal of it will only encourage him to do it more.

— *A.L., 40, white female, Missouri*

We found:

Black comedian Lavell Crawford, best known for playing huge bodyguard Huell on AMC's "Breaking Bad" and its spin-off "Better Call Saul," took time out from being the enemy to speak to us about his menacing ways.

"I'm in a grocery store, say in a small city in Kentucky or Ohio, and being a big black guy, little white kids look at me like 'What in the hell is he doing? What is he doing in our store?'" he said. "You can tell they haven't been around too many brothers."

Crawford says it's usually outside influences — a parent or grandparent — that cause the fear.

"Grandma may make some great brownies, but she may not like black people."

He gets the "full of woe" stare on elevators, too.

"White women, they try to get off, but the door shuts too fast. They look at me like, 'Oh I guess we're all in this together now.' I want to tell them: 'Yeah, I'm just as scared as you are. And I wish I would have gotten off, too, because I did fart when I got on. Enjoy."

A good solution for kids? Don't just pull them aside and tell them what they said was wrong, Crawford suggested. Show them by example. Acclimate them by putting them in situations with people of different ethnic and racial backgrounds.

"I had to learn, too. After watching 'Roots' on TV, I was scared of white folks. I mean, Lord, they cut our feet off," he said. "Then I went to an all-white school, and this white friend Keith invited me to his house. And they were real sweet people."

A gripping question about crotch-holding

They asked:

I notice black men walking around holding their genitals (from outside). Also, I saw a young man holding his pants up with one hand, and the back was under his buttocks. Are these two acts confined to blacks?

— Thomas, 70, white, Jacksonville

You said:

People have to find something to complain about. No one talks about the boys who wear tight pants up to their nipples with suspenders.

— JJ, 15, black female, Detroit

Since 70-plus percent of [rap] music is purchased by suburban white youths, perhaps these are the images that motivate them to buy this music. ... The prison culture inspired the pants that seem to be falling down. Grabbing one's jewels is a symbol of power. Alternatively, comedian Richard Pryor answered that by saying something similar to: "Y'all took everything else. We are just checking to see if they are still there."

— Herb, Atlanta

We found:

Black guys have some sort of toehold on the crotch-hold? Give Italians some credit, too.

Italian dictator Benito Mussolini reportedly did it big-time, long before the King of Pop started tugging. Turns out that publicly manhandling the goods may have started as far back as pre-Christian Roman times, by those who believed it warded off the evil eye (somebody gazing at you to cause you harm). Online magazine Slate featured an article about it, with context from

Pellegrino D'Acierno, professor of Italian Studies at Hofstra University.

In more modern times, associating the crotch-grab with black males is another way to hyper-sexualize them, said writer Jimi Izrael, culture critic and moderator of "The Barbershop" for NPR's "Tell Me More" radio program.

"Everything seems more 'sinister' when black guys do it — dancing, crotch-grabbing, even wearing a baseball cap backward," said Izrael, author of "The Denzel Principle: Why Black Women Can't Find Good Black Men."

"Little Richard grabbed, but so did Jerry Lee Lewis. It's a way to demonize black masculinity ... I acknowledge the gay community, but for some black men, [this is a] way to demonstrate 'I'm proud to be straight, virile, black...' It is silly, yeah, but in the same way that a lot of non-verbal cues are."

And the saggy-pants-in-jail storyline? Revisionist history, he said.

"It's actually from prep culture. Back in the '80s, the white preps wore Polo, and part and parcel of the look was to sag your 501 jeans. It was a small sag then, and it's evolved.

"It's counter-intuitive to attribute it to jailhouse culture. I mean, if you were to wear your pants low, you're going to get [raped] in prison."

Are African-Americans doing a slow (or fast) burn in the sun?

They asked:

Do African-Americans sunburn, and if so, how might it be possible to tell?

— Jeff S., 31, white, Bremerton, Wash.

You said:

LOL, yeah, black people do burn. My mom and I are very dark. She burned and didn't know what was going on. She went through emergency, and they told her she was burned. When I burned, I didn't panic. I just broke out the aloe. We both have to wear sunblock, though.

— Duane, black, Washington, D.C.

We can be albino and blue-black and all the colors in between. The fairer the skin, the more propensity to burn when out in the sun. ... I'm medium brown and my father is two to three shades darker. If out in the sun too long, he burns. I've never gotten sunburned — but I do freckle!

— Kim, black, Minneapolis

Because I'm somewhat fair-skinned, I don't tan well, I burn, and it looks just like when white people get sunburn: red and maybe blistery. The black people I know who are a good amount darker than I am tend to tan rather than burn.

— Jessica, 28, black, Cincinnati

We found:

Blacks can get red the way whites do, but only in a blue moon.

Surveys analyzed by the Centers for Disease Control show that 47 percent of white men and 40 percent of white women reported getting sunburned in the past year. The figures for other racial and ethnic groups: Hispanic blacks — 12.4 percent of men, 9.5 percent

14

of women; Asians/Pacific Islanders —16.2 percent of men, 16.1 percent of women; American Indians/Alaska Natives — 30.4 percent of men, 21.5 percent of women; and non-Hispanic blacks — 5.8 percent of both men and women.

"When I interact with [darker-skinned] patients, they're surprised to learn they can indeed burn," said dermatologist Susan C. Taylor, founder of BrownSkin.net. "But when they think about it, many report, 'Yeah, when I was in Florida or the Caribbean, or in extreme sunlight, I did get a sunburn.' "

The issue often is lack of awareness, she said.

"They can see it and feel it — many people say you can't see the red in black skin, well ... of course you can tell it's red," added Taylor, co-author of "Treatments for Skin of Color." It will be red and tender, but they might pass it off not knowing it's sunburn."

Studies show that on average, African-Americans have a natural Sun Protection Factor (SPF) of about 13, higher than lighter-skinned people due to the level of melanin in their skin, Taylor said.

So, while many paler folks might need a sunscreen with a 30 SPF (recommended by the American Academy of Dermatology), darker-skinned people may need a sunscreen of only about 15 SPF, she added.

"It's important for people of all skin tones to wear sunscreen because of the possibility of burning," Taylor said. "Also, people with darker tones can be troubled by dark marks, known as hyperpigmentation, and often those will darken with sun exposure."

Tag, you're it? Why don't black people cut them off their clothes?

They asked:

Why do black people seem to wear clothes with the tags still on them?

— Chris, Jacksonville

You said:

I've seen guys do this in high school and at my university. It's usually on expensive caps and tennis shoes. To me it's stupid, but obviously they want everybody to know about their expensive whatevers.

— Dee, 19, black female, Dallas

I heard it's done so they can return the item after they wear it.

— JR, 44, black female, Chicago

Dishonest people, not black people, wear clothes and then return them.

— Tresha, 23, black, Atlanta

I see hardly any blacks wearing tags. It's like saying why do whites worship Abercrombie? Those few ignorant individuals you refer to are trying to superficially display the brand for something expensive they can't really afford.

— Peter, black, Jacksonville

What gives you the right to call someone ignorant who wears tags? My aunt does it all the time, and I find her very classy and intelligent.

— N., 14, black female, Baltimore

The only thing I've ever worn with tags were fitted hats. It was the style. It's not just blacks. It's just about anyone into hip-hop fashion.

— Lakeisha, 17, black, Roanoke, Va.

We found:

We left a sticker on once, just to brag. It doesn't work with a Honda Fit.

Leaving tags and stickers on is all about signaling, said Dan Ariely, professor of behavioral economics at Duke University and author of "Predictably Irrational: The Hidden Forces that Shape Our Decisions."

"It's like a peacock: Why does it have that un-useful tail? It's saying, 'Look at me!' It's why men buy red sports cars," Ariely said. "With a price tag, it says 'I have this nice item, plus it's new.' "

A visible tag also shows a lack of symmetry, which brings attention because it doesn't fit expectations, he said. "So it's doing something against the standard."

The practice may have begun in urban areas, though it didn't stay there. People who study trends have found that many of them start in urban, poor areas, Ariely said.

"And rap in general is an anti-cultural sentiment. It's supposed to be rebellious ... like a rapper wearing his jeans low. There are all these small nuances that change rapidly for those who understand what's going on. You want to create a sign that shows you are aware of the changes going on."

She's not big on the black jokes about spankings

They asked:

As a black child, I was beaten as punishment/discipline and so were my friends and relatives. Black comedians often joke about childhood beatings. Why does this seem acceptable?

— T.C., 24, black female, Enterprise, Ala.

You said:

Because most of us who were beat did do something wrong. Mistakes and "bad" things generally lead to negative results. The problem, of course, is that people who get beat the most are people who probably have difficulty controlling themselves or understanding why their behavior is wrong.

— Omelio, 28, black male, Philadelphia

I don't know anyone who thinks child abuse is funny. Who are you hanging out with?

— Dot, Los Angeles

It's fodder for comedy just because it's a shared experience. Nowadays, of course, more and more people can't tell the difference between corporal punishment and child abuse, and of course a fair number won't even recognize there is a difference, so it's not funny to them.

— Jason, 25, white, Bloomington, Ind.

We found:

To see why black comics joke about getting a beating, we called Alonzo Bodden, who won the Season 3 of NBC's "Last Comic Standing" and is a regular on NPR's "Wait Wait…Don't Tell Me!" (More importantly, he's the voice of Thunderon on Power Ranger TV shows and movies).

It's bonding with the audience, he said, because many African-Americans did get spanked or worse.

"But we're not joking about abuse or being scarred for life," he said, they're kidding around about just enough punishment to keep the kids in line before they're too old and won't listen.

"I was disciplined by my folks, and my baby sitter had a razor strap — you'd see that leather hanging on the door and think, 'I don't know what it would take to reach that level, but I don't want to go there.' "

Bodden said he and his friends used to wonder how white kids got away with talking back to their folks, but today he sees a lack of discipline from all parents.

And he disagrees that those who do lay their hands on their kids are only African-American (in fact, some studies show parents who are black, Southern or poorer all use physical punishment at a somewhat higher rate than other parents).

"Believe me, white families laugh at the jokes, too, because they experienced it ... I'm sure there were a lot of ass-whippings in the trailer park, too."

Do blacks wait longer to bury their dead?

They asked:

Why do black Americans wait at least a week after death before burying the deceased?

— *D., 52, white male, Jacksonville*

You said:

A lot of my family is spread across the East Coast. It takes time for those able to attend to get the time off work and travel.

— *Rosemary, black, Nashville*

My mother works at a funeral home. The longer white people sit out after they are dead, they start changing colors.

— *Alicia, 15, black, Atlanta*

Why was the Pope buried four days after his death? Religious statutes. Skin color has nothing to do with it.

— *D.M., 21, black female, Richmond, Va.*

Many blacks depend on insurance policies to finance burial. The insurance company doesn't always distribute the funds in a timely manner; hence the wait. Also, my extended family prefers to celebrate the life of the deceased prior to funeral services.

— *Sherry, 24, black, Bakersfield, Calif.*

It's stupid to base the reason on money. It's because of the skin colors. White people ... are going to begin changing color after death. African-Americans are already brown, and it's not as fast a process.

— *Camille, 18, black, Ohio*

We found:

Yes, we're going to talk about the discoloration stuff. Be patient.

It would be odd for African-Americans to hold a funeral earlier than seven to 10 days after death, with much of that traced to West African traditions, said professor Ronald Barrett, chair of the psychology department at Loyola Marymount University and an expert on African-American funeral customs.

In West Africa, out of respect for the dead, to honor their life and to have time to gather family and relatives, funerals were and still are put off.

This all had a lasting impact once Africans were taken to the U.S. as slaves. Unlike some ethnicities, many black people still view funeral services as "primary rituals," so time is taken to arrange and gather finances, make preparations and inform friends and relatives (often via word of mouth).

Loved ones may be scattered geographically, but "in the African-American tradition ... there's a high communal value in having everyone there," so services are delayed to allow for travel time, Barrett said.

As far as whites getting buried faster because otherwise they might turn a non-whiter shade of pale: Fairer skin in some cases can appear to discolor or darken a bit quicker after death, said Audrey Throckmorton of C.L. Page Mortuary in Jacksonville (although Barrett disagreed).

But, well, there's this thing called embalming, which can give a more natural skin tone for any race.

"We have chemicals and can add dyes with the body fluid," Throckmorton said, "so for white people, it keeps the skin pinkish and more natural, so that's not really an issue."

Black ladies and those lovely, long fake nails

They asked:

Why do black ladies always get fake nails that are so long that they can't even pick change up off the counter or type on a register? They seem ridiculous, and look awful.

— *Julie, 27, Akron, Ohio*

You said:

I've seen white women with the same fake, long nails. Do you find them ridiculous, too?

— *Christelle, Buffalo, N.Y.*

I'm a black male and know exactly what you're saying! I have no idea why they do that. It's disgusting. The real reason: " 'Cause they're trifling."

— *David, black, Columbia, Md.*

What is more "trifling" is someone who labels someone else "trifling" because of their . . . fingernails.

— *Amber, 27, black, Raleigh, N.C.*

How are long nails disgusting? Would you rather them be stubby and have dirt in them and see the imperfections? Which is more disgusting?

— *Lyrick, 20, black female, Washington, D.C.*

The vast majority of black women do not wear long, false fingernails. Since I am a nurse, I know all about the health problems that may arise.

— *Sherry, 26, black, Fort Worth*

I teach at a small college and have observed that about half of my female students wear acrylic nails or get manicures. I think it represents a certain level of "finish" to these students, even if they are otherwise wearing jeans and no makeup.

— *Betsy, 48, white, Cazenovia, N.Y.*

We found:

And now a public health message for all our hospitalized citizens: The nurse in your room? She probably shouldn't be doing her duty with phony nails on, especially if you're lying there in serious condition.

The Centers for Disease Control and the Association of Perioperative Registered Nurses cite studies showing that health care workers with artificial nails are more likely to carry germs on their fingertips.

Both groups strongly urge that nurses nix nifty non-natural nails.

Regarding fashion, long artificial nails are about style, which is about artistic expression, which for some African-Americans is about making a personal statement in the face of oppression and even invisibility, said Holly Alford, a fashion professor at Virginia Commonwealth University who researches urban style.

"During slavery, you were told you couldn't wear certain things," she said. "The way you dress says a lot about you, your age, your status. . . . Look at men of color: Even Quincy Jones says that 'With all my money, I still feel a need to dress like this [stylish] to express who I am so people treat me as equal.' "

Long fake nails also can mean being on the front lines of style.

"We've had a lot of obstacles. But one thing we can do is be on the forefront of fashion," said Alford, who called her own artificial nails more on the "reasonable" side in length. "Black women may be thinking, 'If you aren't going to listen to me, you'll definitely see me,' And let's get real: With those [very long] nails, you can't help but notice."

Alford disagreed that long fake nails are a class issue, but said they might be an age issue.

"Take the older generation. My mother will look at someone's long nails and think, 'What the hell is she thinking of? Oh my God!' "

23

She wants to aks them a question

They asked:

Why do so many black people say "aks"? I grew up saying "basghetti" and "liberry," but I don't still do it.

— FreedaBee, 42, white female, California

You said:

A small mix of dialect with a lot of ignorance. The same reason a lot of (mostly) white people come to my job and "ask" about inkjet "cartilages."

— Brad, 33, black, Winchester, Va.

As long as people understand what we are saying, it doesn't matter how we say it.

— Jalissa and Charles, both 18, Chicago

I wonder this myself and am not proud. Speak proper English, my fellow Afro-Americans!

— Cliff, 33, black, San Francisco

Most black folks migrated from the South, so since we tend to be raised in households with Southern speech patterns, we tend to speak that way, too.

— Jim, 32, black, Jones, Ohio

Not everyone pronounces words like Caucasians do, and it's not right to expect them to. There are differences among us, including family rearing, foods, clothing styles, hairstyles, etc. Why would speech pattern be any different?

— Amber, 27, black, Raleigh, N.C.

We found:

Some might akseth: If it was OK for the "Father of English literature," isn't it OK for some black people (or anyone else)?

Chaucer employed it during the Middle English period ("I axe, why the fyfte man Was nought housband to the Samaritan?" — Wife of Bath's Prologue, circa 1386).

For a while (as in centuries), both forms were accepted. But around 1600, hoity-toity types in the Old Country decided "aks" t'weren't good enough.

"However, 'aks' was the form most commonly used in the dialect of English that slaves were exposed to," said Sandra Wilde, Professor of Childhood Education at Hunter College in Manhattan, who researched the issue for her book "What's a Schwa Sound Anyway? A Holistic Guide to Phonetics, Phonics, and Spelling."

"It's the nature of language to change, but one reason black English has persisted has to do with social separation. . . . You speak like the people you hang with — and there is still a fair degree of social separation in our culture based on race."

So "aks" really isn't "worse" or "lazier," it's just that some people retained this older version, she said. In fact, one reason for African-American Vernacular English (Ebonics) is that people who've been marginalized often hold onto language to retain their identity.

John McWhorter, associate professor of English and Comparative Literature at Columbia University and a linguistics expert, wrote about the phenomenon of people talking a certain way primarily to express who they are – perhaps even unbeknownst to themselves.

In an LA. Times essay, he noted that for black people, Aks just has a different meaning than Ask:

"Words are more than sequences of letters, and 'ax' is drunk in from childhood," he writes. "'Ax" is a word indelibly associated not just with asking but with black people asking. That sentiment alone is powerful enough to cut across conscious decisions about what is standard or proper. 'Ax,' then, is as integral a part of being a black American as are subtle aspects of carriage, demeanor, humor and religious practice."

25

Hispanic immigrants catch a break from U.S. blacks

They asked:

How do African-Americans feel about all the Hispanics coming into the United States?

— *Lindsay, 19, North Carolina*

You said:

I don't care who is coming to this country. At some point, we all had to migrate here or be brought or sent here.

— *Tanaira, 16, Baltimore*

We don't have a problem as long as the following criteria are met: Please check in at the door. Please understand the economics here. There have to be enough jobs, food and social services to go around. Please understand you aren't the only people immigrating here. I don't understand why Mexicans feel they deserve special treatment over all other peoples. Please don't blow the Mexican flag in our face and expect us to accept this. And please drop the "You have it, we don't, so just give it to us" mentality.

— *C., black male, Michigan*

I don't have a problem with Hispanic immigrants . . . but I, like most Americans, believe illegal aliens regardless of nationality don't belong here. I don't understand why they have rights in the first place.

— *Peter, black, Jacksonville*

I feel fine with it. A few of my friends are Hispanic, and I love 'em to death.

— *Lakeisha, 17, black, Virginia*

We found:

U.S. blacks view immigration slightly more favorably than whites do (Gallup poll). The percentage of blacks who feel undocumented immigrants should receive social services is twice that of whites, and black people in general strongly believe immigrants are hard-working with solid family values (Pew Center poll).

However, just to be complex, the Pew Center also found that a higher percentage of blacks say they or a family member lost a job or didn't get one because of an immigrant, and that blacks more often feel immigrants take jobs from U.S. citizens.

"You do see concerns that the political and economic agenda of African-Americans will be left behind, and you do see some anti-Latino stereotyping . . . though that is not different from the general public," said Eric Ward, former national field director for the Center for New Community in Chicago, which tracks anti-immigrant activity.

"It doesn't help black America to blame immigrants. . .. When people are arming themselves, patrolling streets and challenging people for proof of citizenship, that should send a chill into everyone."

While there are regional examples of job competition with immigrants — meat and poultry processing in the South, for example — overall, many jobs once thought of as "black jobs" in manufacturing or service sectors have already been off-shored, Ward   noted.

"There's a misconception that we've [blacks] been put in a race with Latinos for the economic bottom . . . and that has limited the conversation on the idea that every job should be a living-wage job in society."

More African-Americans are seeing that being anti-immigration is not useful, he said, and that "every good movement for justice lifts up everyone."

Do blacks have a taste for Chinese fare?

They asked:

It seems that in America, black people are crazy about Chinese food. What are the cultural reasons behind this?

— Tom I., white, 34, Paris

You said:

It's for the same reason Chinese people in America love McDonald's: it is quick, inexpensive and tasty.

— Michele, 38, white, Jacksonville

Chinese food is just good as hell!

— Nyla, 17, black, New Jersey

Chinese food tastes good to lots of folks. I see many Hispanics whenever I go to a Chinese restaurant.

— E.D., 48, black, Missouri

I never ate rice without sugar until I moved up North. My first taste of fried rice hooked me for life. It was bought at the corner rice house, where most African-Americans buy and prefer.

— Vivian, 56, black, Houston

We do spend money on good food — that's why we encourage the Greeks, the Japanese and others to bring their cuisines to the ghetto ... they'll get rich! We would love to have other foods in our community, but for the time being, we are fighting just to get grocery stores.

— Diane, black, Charlotte, N.C.

We found:

Truth is that eating preferences vary just as much among African-Americans as any other group, says Eric J. Bailey, professor of medical anthropology at East Carolina University and author of "Food Choice and Obesity in Black America."

That said, as major cities developed in the United States, various ethnic groups did find themselves in proximity to one another, among them Chinese and black people. That led to mixing and matching of cuisines, Bailey said. And consider Chinese food's similarity to soul food: basic food products that are altered with extra sauces to be made sweet or spicy.

"Soul food was developed that way, too. By adding sauces to stuff that was bland, it began a pattern of modifying food. Slaves had to find a way to use the remnants left behind by their owners. You try to make whatever is available usable and tasteful for the palate. You experiment ... when you're given scraps, you're going to try to make it nice for everyone."

And like soul food, Chinese food, with its fresh ingredients like vegetables and some meat sautéed in for good measure, can and should be changed to make it better for the body.

"We can still adhere to the pattern, but we can use sodium substitutes or find other ways to affect things like the amount of cholesterol," he said. "We can maintain the feel, but make it healthier."

Is use of Sheneneh just a nay-nay?

They asked:

If someone is upset with you and waving their hand with fingers outstretched in the air a few inches from your face, is it considered racist to say "You need to stop going all Shanaynay on me"?

— *Kay, white, Jacksonville*

You said:

That would be racist regardless of what the other person was doing. Obviously, the use of the name Shanaynay refers to the sometimes creative names of African-Americans. If you said "Star Jones" instead of "Shanaynay," it might be different because Star is a particular person known for certain things and you could mean "You need to stop buying all those Payless shoes."

— *F., white female, California*

That's been out of style since the show "Martin," which featured the character "Shenaenae."

— *Lynne H., Louisville, Ky.*

If I was doing that to someone, and then they said something like that, I'd probably burst out laughing. That being said, I probably would never say that unless I was joking around with my friends.

— *Cassy, 22, white, Jacksonville*

Would this even be an issue if I was mimicking, say, an Italian gesture and saying "Don't get all Mario on me?" As an outsider to America, I think black people seem to be hypersensitive about the color of their skin. In Australia I think we understand that . . . there are generalizations that are true to certain cultures and/or races, and it's fine to poke fun at people as long as it's done in a non-aggressive way.

— *Jason G., Australian, Germany*

We found:

Du-uh, it's Sheneneh, not Shanaynay or Shenaenae. (OK, we confess we hadn't heard of her, either.)

"She" was actually a he, a "ghetto girl" portrayed by Martin Lawrence on the Fox sitcom "Martin" in the mid-'90s. Sheneneh Jenkins was a sassy, stereotypically over-the-top character who shouted phrases like "Oh no you di-in't!"

So here's the key, said John R. Rickford, professor of linguistics at Stanford University and author of "Spoken Soul: The Story of Black English": Is the phrase in question being used in a general way to try to paint African-Americans with a broad brush, or is it referring to the specific character on Martin?

If the latter, that absorbs a bit of the sting on the offensiveness scale, he said. But let's say the person had thrown out a "creative-sounding" name not tied to a TV character (may we humbly suggest "LaShaquanda," a respondent to a different question on our website). "In that case, she might be disparaging an aspect of black cultural behavior in general," Rickford said. "If she's talking to a black person and says that, it would be interpreted as a put-down."

He stressed there were no "hard-and-fast" rules, because context is so important — though there is still "a lot of sensitivity of boundaries between black and white styles."

"It's not like a committee sits down and says this is OK and this isn't ... it's hard to draw a line."

A flake by any other name would still be dandruff

They asked::

Do black people get dandruff? And if they do, what color is it? I've asked my black friends this, but they think I'm joking and just laugh.

— Clint, 32, white, Jacksonville

You said:

I have to admit, I laughed, too.

— E.D., 48, black female, Kansas City, Mo.

Hold onto your shorts, junior; here's a fact that may shake your world loose: When you look at somebody's skin, you're looking at a layer of colorless cells. The skin pigment is deeper than the surface. When this layer dries and flakes off, it appears white.

— Nick F., Seattle

Are black people not human?

— Peter, 21, black, Jacksonville

Yes, black people get dandruff. It is more a gray color because a black person's skin gets a grayish hue when it is very dry (which is where the term "ashy" comes from). Most blacks put "grease" on their scalps to avoid this. In case you are wondering, I didn't know any of this until I met and married a black man.

— Darby, 33, white, New York

Our dandruff looks like tar flakes. Just kidding, it's white and flaky.

— Cris, black female, Michigan

When I get dandruff, it looks white on my black clothes and dark on my white clothes.

— David, black, London

We may not get it as often because we don't wash our hair as often, but I know we get it. I have some right now.

— Monika, 27, black, Houston

Because of the texture of our hair, the dandruff usually stays in our hair, instead of falling onto our clothing.

— Alisha, 36, black, Charlotte

We found:

We don't mean to get under anyone's skin, but apparently some black people do, in fact, have chips on their shoulders.

Relax, we're talking about seborrheic dermatitis here, after all.

Monica Farrow of Jacksonville, an expert on African-American hair, confirmed it.

"The skin is an organ that sheds, and we all have skin," said Farrow, who runs OurHair.net, which offers care solutions for African-American and ethnic hair. "Dandruff is nothing more than shedding skin. If you're human, you do get dandruff."

But it may be harder to see on some people.

"A lot of black people use moisturizers with oil on their scalps because black hair can be more naturally dry," she said. "The oil tends to disguise the fact that the dandruff is there [because] when oil is on the scalp, the flakes that can fall become translucent."

Because oils attract dirt, many African-Americans are experimenting with "no-oil routines," using emulsions and creams that are higher in water content, Farrow said.

Still, nothing can fully guarantee against an occasional bout of the scaly scurf.

"Oh yeah, we get it," she said. "When I grew up, we had Selsun Blue in the shower."

Is it black and white when it comes to the potty?

They asked:

Why do white people potty train their kids so late, while black people train them earlier?

— *Lynn, Memphis, Tenn.*

You said:

Probably because more white women have the time to wipe their babies' bottoms than many black women have the privilege to, between three jobs, rising out of poverty and generations of slavery.

— *Daryl, 30, Asian, Texas*

It's also very common in Europe and the former Soviet Union to potty train early (12 months or so). This could be because diapers are expensive.

— *Kate, 34, white, Columbia, Md.*

Pacifiers, bottles, breast-feeding and diapers are areas we black mothers tend to want to rid our children of as early as possible because they weigh the child down. Having a 3-year-old hooked on a pacifier is like having a 3-year-old hooked on crack. I guess we also think it's hard enough for black kids to progress in America, so why keep them attached to unnecessary "baby things"? We tend to want our children far less dependent on us as soon as possible because sometimes life has a way of happening, and we don't want to leave behind dependent children.

— *Raquel, 33, black, Houston*

I never recognized any correlation between race and potty-training. I do think, however, that stingy people or those with lower incomes are more likely to potty train early because day care for potty-trained infants is easier to find and significantly cheaper.

— *Kristina, 23, black, Washington*

We found:

When controversy like this rears its possibly dirty behind (we aren't checking — you do it), there's only one option: seek out the "Potty Pro."

Teri Crane, known by that moniker for having helped thousands of parents in her "potty training boot camps," is author of "Potty Train Your Child in Just One Day" (Simon & Schuster).

"I can tell you, emphatically, this is not a black or white thing. Black people don't do it [potty train their kids] before white people. It's based on the needs of the individual child."

Cheli English-Figaro, co-founder of the Mocha Moms support group for mothers of color, agreed.

"I've never heard anything like that — us taking shorter time to train our kids," she said. "Now, my mom did train me by age 1, but that was the cultural norm for everyone back in the mid-'60s. Before Pampers and diaper services, you had to wash your own cloth diapers, and people didn't want to deal with that for too long."

While some cultures do train their children early — tribes in East Africa have had success using a "soothing, calm approach" to train their offspring by as young as 5 months — today in America it's generally not recommended to start training until at least age 2, Crane said. Meanwhile, the American Academy of Family Physicians and the American Academy of Pediatrics give no "set" date, but both say many children don't show "readiness" until 18 to 24 months.

Is lifting kids by the arms a racial issue?

They asked:

Why do African-American women pick up their babies by one arm? Are they aware they can dislocate the shoulder?

— Becky, Jacksonville

You said:

I hate anyone picking up a young child like that, and I do not pay attention to the race of the offender. My mother has always said the same thing: she hates to see that, too.

— Moni, black, Fort Myers

I've seen women of many different cultures do this. I am guilty of it. I have 20-month-old triplet cousins, and when I'm caring for them and two want to be picked up and you're trying to get things done, I swing them up on my hip. I've never done it to an infant because you can hurt them, but toddlers are more "durable."

— Asia D., 21, black, Phoenix

The black females you've seen doing this are usually the single, very young, untrained "baby's mommas" who are too ignorant of proper child care or too stubborn to learn. By the way, I've seen this done by black and white single mothers.

— Brad, black, Winchester, Va.

We found:

Rest assured the country isn't crawling with kids in pain because their moms yanked on their arms and dislocated their shoulders.

Subluxated their elbows? Sure.

"It's called nursemaid's elbow," said Denise Dowd, chief of injury prevention at Children's Mercy Hospital in Kansas City, Mo. "You

can pull the bone out of place. You'll know something's wrong because the kid will not use the arm — it'll hang there."
Such a partial dislocation, mostly caused by someone tugging hard on or pulling the child up by one arm, usually has to be put back in place in the emergency room.

"We twist the arm back in. There's no medication. We see it hundreds of times a year."

It's not restricted to African-American kids, she said.

"It can happen to anyone; pediatricians don't typically teach parents about it."

Wilma Ann Anderson's point, exactly.

The publisher of Mahogany Baby Web-zine for black parents, and a mother of four, Anderson says lack of education is the likely culprit when parents err with their offspring.

"I don't see it as an African-American thing. Folks in general do what they know. If you haven't been introduced to new ways of doing things, then it's very uncommon you would start implementing these things."

Black parents do tend to discipline more harshly than white parents, she said, but it varies from person to person.

"It's been a theme passed down for generations among black families, and it's biblically based . . . that it's OK to be physical with the child when reprimanding. But many black families are going against that, using the white mom 'timeout' system — which I personally thought I never would use, but I said 'Hey, let me give it a try.' You implement what works."

Tattoo you: White ink will fade on dark skin

They asked:

Because people with light skin get tattoos with black or colored inks, why don't black people get tattoos with white ink?

— *Jean T., Shreveport, La.*

You said:

White ink exists, and I've seen it on some tattoos, but it is quite transparent, more so even than other light-colored tattoo inks, and is mostly used to lighten the overlying skin tone and achieve something approximating "pale." Therefore, on a very dark-skinned black person, white ink would at best lighten the overlying skin a few tones, and in many cases wouldn't show at all.

— *Ann, 38, white, Kansas City, Mo.*

The first misconception a lot of people have is that if someone is of African descent, they have dark, black skin. Skin hues can range from rather light to extremely dark. So for a large amount of people, a tattoo done in black ink shows up just as well on their skin as it does on any other ethnicity. Even on basic dark skin, black ink still shows, just not with as much contrast. Traditionally, tattoos were done in either blue or black. Personally, from what I've seen, when black won't show up, people use blue instead. I'm not sure if maybe white ink is less reliable, or if it is just too vivid, but I have rarely seen it used outside of a "picture scene" type of tattoo.

— *A.S., 27, female, Idaho*

We found:

We wanted to track down someone with a tattoo on the small of their back or side of their ankle but had a hard time locating Everyone and His Mother.

We opted for Roni Zulu, L.A.-based tattoo artist to the stars, who is also African-American.

He says a white tattoo on dark skin would at first look tight — but later just wouldn't pass the color test.

Tattoo ink is deposited through the layers of the skin, says Zulu, who has marked up such heavyweights as Janet Jackson, Dennis Rodman, Rosie O'Donnell, Lisa Bonet, David Duchovny and Queen Latifah.

As the tattoo heals, the top layers of skin exfoliate and grow back with no pigment, leaving only the bottom layers retaining ink.

"Whenever you see a tattoo, you are actually looking through that person's top layers of skin and viewing the tattoo underneath," he said.

Because brown skin is less transparent than light skin, a whitish tattoo just wouldn't show up well under the new dark layers.

"After a few weeks you end up with a stack of brown skin on top of the tattoo. So dark-skinned people say 'What the heck happened to my bright tattoo?' "

Dark ink works better, though often it still ends up looking "a little greenish" beneath dark skin, Zulu said. Some African-Americans, especially in fraternities, go for scarification instead because the raised scars stand out more than tattoos.

And while many mainstream American blacks had veered away from their African history and culture, which includes scarification and tattoos, they have warmed to the idea of body marks again, notably with African symbols, Zulu said.

"Unfortunately, most of it [tattooing] still exists in gangland . . . that stigma still floats around in black society."

Stop touching me! Getting personal about personal space

They asked:

Most people accept being bumped into as part of living in a busy metropolis. But every time I bump into a black person, they get extremely upset and start yelling. What's up with this?

— Mark, 49, white, New York

You said:

Blacks have a greater sense of personal space and take it as an aggressive act to bump into someone and then not apologize.

— G., 43, black male, Phoenix

It may be the way people treat some blacks: as if our feelings don't matter, or as if a little annoyance here and there isn't a big thing.

— Christine, black, Hartford, Conn.

Many blacks know whites are basically afraid of them. They like to intimidate you and probably would back off if you became aggressive.

— Sam, white, Fort Myers

Black folks have so many issues with white folks that the last thing they want is some white dude bumping into them who doesn't have the manners to apologize.

— Bella, 33, Afro-Caribbean, Washington, D.C.

We found:

To talk about folks caroming off each other in the Big Apple, we phoned Miami Herald columnist Leonard Pitts, an African-American known to comment on race and culture in America in a Pulitzer Prize-winning sort of way.

Using race as the chief variable for who gets miffed when jostled is dubious, Pitts argues, because it's just one characteristic — albeit the most visible — among many that differentiate people, including class, education and upbringing.

Yet there may be something to what some dub the "black tax" — an extra burden African-Americans shoulder just for being black, piled onto all the usual worries like kids, high gas prices, a jerk boss, etc.

"It demands an extra pound of flesh . . . so there can be an undercurrent of anger in some African-Americans, where they expect the worst until shown differently."

But other minorities have obstacles, too, no?

"Let's just say my forebears came here to oppression, whereas other minorities came here to escape it.

"We [blacks] are trying to make a life among those who oppressed us. It's like going through a bitter divorce but still being in the same bed."

Are black women less anxious about their weight?

They asked:

Why do overweight black women exude self-confidence, while most white overweight women hate themselves?

— *Jennie, 22, white, W.Va.*

You said:

Big hips, chests and behinds are prized among most black men.

— *K.J., 17, black female, Bronx, N.Y.*

I think African-American women are stronger. They've overcome the most trials and prejudice. I'm tired of society having unrealistic concepts of what women should look like.

— *Cyndi, 28, white female, Ohio*

White women miss out on good food, warm sun and daring dress styles by letting others define their beauty. Confidence comes from inside, when you realize you will never be what fashion magazines want but can still acknowledge you are "all that" because you look in the mirror and can see it.

— *Mrs. Williams, 26, Athens, Ga.*

Enough about how confident we are. In a minute I'll have to pull out my boots. Let's stop pretending black women don't have self-image issues. Before we can heal, we have to admit we hurt. That always-strong, sexy, intelligent persona is not a realistic portrait of who I am.

— *Zawadi, 34, Michigan*

I tried to fool myself with that "I'm big and beautiful" nonsense — right up till I broke the zipper out of a pair of size-14 pants. Using cute terms will not erase the truth that too many of us are just too damn big. And trust me, the majority of overweight sistas are not feeling the confidence they exude.

— *Rhonda, 42, black, Laurelton, N.Y.*

We found:

To approach the topic with a sense of dignity, we spoke with Biggest Loser reality TV star Andrea Baptiste, a black woman who lost a bunch of weight off her hump and off her trunk — in the back and in the front.

"Norms in society are based on a Hollywood version of beauty that is not a black woman. It's Lindsay Lohan, lean, tone — and white," said Baptiste, a motivational speaker. "Black women grew up with curvy women as an image of beauty, in Jet and Vibe."

Without pressure to be thin, and with many black men preferring "meat on the bones," black women can feel better about their bodies, she said.

"White women want to fit in, but we're more like 'Screw it, if you don't like it, move on.'"

Being large and in charge, however, doesn't mean taking health for granted, and nowadays more black women appreciate eating right, exercising and watching their cholesterol and blood pressure, she said.

"Plenty of overweight black women are quite content with who they are. But plenty, myself, too, weren't happy being big. Still, it's not about doing it to please others. White women: Love yourselves first. Forget what others think. And eat something. Have a rib."

What's in a name? Discussing distinctively black monikers

They asked:

Why do African-American children always have names most people have never heard of?

— *Lizzie, 72, white, Jacksonville*

You said:

I guess you forgot about Gwyneth Paltrow's child, Apple. And Demi Moore has daughters named Rumer, Scout and Tallulah.

— *Sharon, black, Clinton Township, Mich.*

For many years African-Americans had to acknowledge names given by slavemasters. Now many African-American are developing their own identity since many have lost a connection with their African culture.

— *Teresa, 30, black, Detroit*

I, too, scratch my head when I hear these crazy names. When you meet a black girl named Sharquita, you're dealing with someone whose parents are scarring their child in a feeble attempt to be unique.

— *Rick, 32, black, Atlanta*

I didn't hear a strange name for a black person until I moved to Florida. Now I'm surrounded by Laquisha, Vshati and Latiera. It's silly. Will we ever have a Secretary of State named Vshati?

— *Jessica, white, Florida*

I guess you forgot our former Secretary of State: Condoleezza.

— *Peter, 21, black, Jacksonville*

We found:

White University of Chicago economist Steven Levitt (he of the best-selling "Freakonomics") and black Harvard race scholar

Roland Fryer wrote a paper in 2003 titled The Causes and Consequences of Distinctively Black Names.

Such names took hold in the early '70s, they reported, as a holdover of the Black Power movement, whose main mission was to stress African culture and beat down the notion of black inferiority.

To take the issue a giant step further, however, they mined the rich birth-certificate data of every Californian born since 1961 — each child's name and race, and their parents' marital status, level of education, ZIP codes and hospital bill payment method.

They found that those most likely to give a child an unusual black name were unmarried, low-income, undereducated teen mothers from black neighborhoods. In Fryer's opinion, the names are given to show solidarity with the black community. (The "blackest" names? Imani, Ebony and Shanice for girls, and DeShawn, DeAndre and Marquis for boys. The "whitest"? Molly, Amy and Claire for girls, and Jake, Connor and Tanner for boys.)

But do blacks with non-"Dick and Jane" names have worse life outcomes on average? Well, yes, but not because of their names, the researchers found.

As they wrote: "If two black boys, Jake Williams and DeShawn Williams, are born in the same neighborhood and into the same familial and economic circumstances, they would likely have similar life outcomes. But the kind of parents who name their son Jake don't tend to live in the same neighborhoods or share economic circumstances with the kind of parents who name their son DeShawn. And that's why, on average, a boy named Jake will tend to earn more money and get more education than a boy named DeShawn. ... DeShawn's name is an indicator — but not a cause — of his life path."

Are you faster or stronger because of your race?

They asked:

Is there a physical difference between the races that would allow certain races to perform better at certain sports? For example, how many world-class sprinters are white?

— Casey, 22, white, Reston, Va.

You said:

It is not PC to suggest genetic differences between races. You are starting to think outside the box the U.S. media has established for us.

— Sid, 34, white, Birmingham, Ala.

To excel in sports requires enormous work. Searching for a racial anatomical difference belittles the training and practice these athletes undergo. After black sprinters began to win races, the press mused that perhaps blacks were good at sprinting, but that whites were better suited for distance running. Then blacks began to win marathons. The old myths developed to explain away black successes do not stand up to analysis.

— R. Stewart, black, Chicago

We found:

Whenever someone claims black athletes are faster than white ones, we know folks will run (some very slowly) to us for facts.

Pundits, including some sports columnists, say speed is all about hard work and dedication. That it's goofy or worse to say genetics play a role.

But we're not talking about pitting average Joes against each other in the 100. We are talking, according to researcher Jon Entine, only about elite athletes.

Entine, a journalist and research fellow at George Mason University, pored over scientific studies for his book "Taboo: Why Black Athletes Dominate Sports and Why We're Afraid to Talk About It (Public Affairs)." He learned that different subgroups of people developed different body characteristics over time relative to their terrain and living conditions.

"It's not an issue of race, it's about population genetics," Entine said. "Certain body types tend to do better in certain sports than others. It's not controversial unless you put it in racial terms."

For example, West Africans tend to have more-developed fast-twitch muscles (necessary for fast burst activity), less body fat, longer arms and legs relative to the torso, and smaller lung capacity (for greater sprinting efficiency). Eurasian peoples have bigger torsos and shorter arms, which makes them better at strength events such as weightlifting. And on and on with other groups.

Entine's critics say performance differences among the so-called "races" fall along cultural and environmental lines, and that using genetics as the primary reason discounts individual effort, opportunity, self-image, discipline, interests and expectations.

Yes, Entine responds, individual athletes of any race can perform at top levels in various sports if they work hard, have great coaching and use their smarts. But some groups of people on average are more suited to certain sports and tend to do better at the very highest levels, where a tenth of a second is a huge difference.

"The truth is that 494 of the top 500 100-meter times in the world are held by a person of central West African ancestry."

Say it loud: I'm black and I'm ... loud?

They asked:

Why do black people act louder in public more than any other race?
— *Sparky, 48, Asian female, Florida*

You said:

I'm not loud in public. My family and friends aren't. The funny thing is, when white people are being loud I hardly notice it, or I respond by saying that those "people" are being loud, rather than those "white people" are being loud. We live in a society where "white" is the norm and anyone who is non-white stands out in every respect.

— *Lash, 24, black female, San Francisco*

Some lower-class black people (and lower-class white people co-opting black culture) use noise to draw attention to themselves and challenge authority. Ridiculously loud laughing, screeching or yelling insults to one another creates a situation in which if one approaches them, their posture is confrontational by default. It is an American trait. Never have I seen a Nigerian woman run up the aisle of a movie theater with her friend in tow because something they'd seen was simply too funny.

— *Austin, 31, white male, Frankfort, Ky.*

I've always wondered why Asian people are so quiet.
— *Sherry, 24, black female, Bakersfield, Calif.*

My friends and I are not quiet. I am shy when I am in a new environment, but when I am with my friends, I am loud. Well, I guess fobs (fresh off the boat) are more quiet. One of my fob friends told me she doesn't want people to tease her broken English or accent.

— *Jo, Asian female, Chino Hills, Calif.*

Everyone gets loud when they're around their friends. Geeky white nerds even get loud and excited when they're talking about science.
— *Alicia, 15, black female, Atlanta*

We found:

We get the "all blacks are loud" catch-all query a lot, and its classic variant, "Why do black people hoot and holler at the movies?"

Most people who complain about boisterous public behavior are older people upset with groups of younger people of any race, says Brenda Rhodes Miller, author of "The Church Ladies' Divine Desserts and Sweet Recollections" (Putnam).

"Young people are loud in situations where they feel uncertain or fearful," she says. "The noise is because they don't want people to mess with them."

As for acting up in the movie theater, while members of any race certainly do this, participatory "loud talk" among some African-Americans can share characteristics of the call and response tradition of many worship services, says Miller, wife of a Baptist minister. They may share their feelings with the group about what they're experiencing, as in church, or even talk back to the characters on-screen, as in "You better watch your back!" or "Look at that fool going into a dark building in the middle of the night!"

"And if you already think black people [do this more], you're going to notice the loud voices more than the black person who tells the others 'Will you please be quiet?'"

The O.U.T.L.O.U.D.
Method to Dialogue

OPEN UP: This is mostly about opening up to yourself. Why do you want to engage someone? Is it for the right reasons? The answers might help you figure out how to approach another person. A friend once told me the real reason I started Y? wasn't for me to learn more about "Buddhists in Asia or lesbians in San Francisco," but because I wanted to learn something more about myself. He was right. Acknowledging that has helped give me perspective when considering others' answers.

USE YOUR HEAD: Plan for the right question. Not all questions need to be the "wet dogs" variety. Stereotypes and clichés don't work as well as sincere attempts to talk.

TIME IT RIGHT: Create the "O.U.T.L.O.U.D. Moment". Pick your spots for provocative dialogue. Find a genuine opening rather than create a false one. It's often during those down times between all the "vital" discourse that we can most easily find a direct path to someone's point of view. If you spend enough time sitting in the cubicle next to someone of a different culture, chances are there'll come a time — over food, perhaps, or during a power outage — when the topic you've been dying to broach will wend its way naturally into the discussion.

LOCK IN ON THE TARGET: Keeping things simple can give the best chance for getting another's trust and a meaningful reply. Some of the best questions at Y?, those that prompt the most telling answers, are also often the easiest to digest. Remember, it's not about winning your point. It's what comes from the heart that counts most — and captures people's interest. Talking from the heart also means easing into things by letting someone know *why* it would help you to learn the answer to your question before you ask it.

OWN UP TO ASSUMPTIONS: One of the most refreshing and repetitive surprises of the Y? project is the difficulty in predicting how a person will respond to a question. Blacks do not think in lockstep. Nor do whites. Nor Christians or Muslims. Nor

50

gays or straights. Be receptive to another's ideas. Wipe the slate clean and listen to the content of the message, not the color or culture of the messenger.

UNLOAD YOUR EXPECTATIONS: Many of us are thinner-skinned than we'll admit. When we get hit with an answer or comment we hadn't anticipated, our emotions can often get caught off-balance, and our egos get bruised. The solution: Expect the unexpected. You'll never be blindsided or taken aback by information that doesn't gibe with your worldview.

DIGEST THE DIALOGUE: Learning about others doesn't stop when the talking's over. Assess what you're told and how it fits with or departs from your perspectives. Recap your discussion with a third party to distill the most relevant information into its most meaningful points.

ABOUT THE AUTHOR

Phillip J. Milano is the founder of Y? The National Forum on People's Differences, the acclaimed cross-cultural dialogue project that encourages people to ask unflinching, politically incorrect questions about our differences.

Since its creation in 1998, Phillip's web site, YForum.com, has attracted millions of visitors and thousands of questions and answers. He has been featured on CBS, CNN, BET and the BBC, and in numerous newspapers, including The Washington Post, New York Times and USA Today.

He is the author of the Perigee book "I Can't Believe You Asked That!" as well as writer of the pioneering newspaper column/blog "Dare to Ask."

Mr. Milano is a 25-year newspaper veteran. He received his Masters of Business Administration from Northern Illinois University and his Bachelors of Science in Journalism from Southern Illinois University.

SPEECHES AND APPEARANCES

Mr. Milano is an in-demand speaker. For bookings, contact

Contemporary Issues Agency
809 Turnberry Drive, Waunakee, WI 53597-2256
Phone: 800-843-2179
Fax: 608-849-6311
CIAspeakers.com
Info@CIAspeakers.com